Don Rittner

Watervliet

Historic Images

ISBN: 9-780937-666647

Dedicated to Jennifer Rittner

Book design by Don Rittner

New Netherland Press
Schenectady, NY

First Edition

Introduction

For some unknown reason there have not been a great number of histories written about the city of Watervliet and those earlier communities that came before it from the 17th to 19th centuries. Certainly much history was made and it is about time that it is conveyed to a welcoming citizenry.

For thousands of years Native Americans made this their home. The first inhabitants of the area that interacted with the first European visitors were the Mohicans, Algonquian speaking Native Americans who were eventually forced out of the land by the interaction of the Iroquois to the west over fur trading rights in the early 17th century and the encroaching Europeans who realized the abundance of resources available in the region.

In 1630, Dutch diamond merchant Killean Van Rennselaer purchased the land that makes up the area that later became the present city of Watervliet. Originally manorial farms it made Van Rennsselaer and his associates wealthy at the expense of those hardy Dutch settlers who worked the land and paid part of their hard work to the Patroon for the "right" to work and live on his land.

One of the first European settlers in Watervliet was Phillip Petersie Schuyler who built the Schuyler Mansion in the south of the city, now known as Schuyler Flats. Others followed and created villages like Washington and Gibbonsville (both incorporated in 1824), Port Schuyler (incorporated in 1827), West Troy (incorporated in 1836) and finally combining them all into the city of Watervliet in 1896.

This collection of images over the centuries brings to light some of the people, events, and institutions that made Watervliet an important and early manufacturing center in the Capital District. This first volume presents Watervliet's streetscapes: scenes from the many businesses, manufacturers, and mom and pop establishments that give the city this rich history. Many old timers will remember many of the stories each picture presents and provide to the younger reader a historical context to where they live and call home. Rather than reinvent the wheel, two previously published short histories of the Town and City of Watervliet are included from a well-written Bicentennial History of Albany by Howell and Tenney and titled "History of the County of Albany, N.Y., from 1609 to 1886." This history was published by W.W. Munsell & Co publishers in New York in 1886. The twentieth century and beyond is being researched and promoted by the wonderful volunteers of the Watervliet Historical Society who gave me permission to sort through their collections and present this overview history for the public. Be sure to support the Society here: https:// watervliethistoricalsociety.org/

Special thanks to Watervliet City Historian and President of the Watervliet Historical Society Tom Ragosta and his wife Marylou, Rosemary Nicols, and to John Cehowski for lighting the idea.

Don Rittner

Streetscapes

The following photographs show Watervliet streets, avenues and byways, and the many retail, wholesale and manufacturing companies along with many residences that made up the early communities that is present day Watervliet. Many of these structures and even streets are gone the way of the wrecking ball, fires, or massive urban renewal projects of the past. Watervliet had its highest population in the first half of the 20th century growing from 4,572 in 1840 to 16,116 by 1940. Its current population is just under 10,000 (9,900). What seemed a death knell to the city came in the early 1970s when the State of New York built Interstate I-787 through most of the city's downtown area that bordered the Hudson River. It has never really recovered from this ill conceived highway project. The following images reveal a once vibrant city and inhabitants that many current old timers will enjoy and remember and for younger generations to ponder.

Emery's Grocery in Port Schuyler. Northeast corner of 3rd Ave and 5th St and 2nd Ave and 3rd St. Delivery car. Corner grocery stores were common before the large supermarket chains became popular. Others were Sam Roda's, Budini, Valente's Cash Market, Hancel's, Christie's, Midway Market, Stebbins, Tartaglia's New Sanitary Market (nicknamed "Dirty Ernie's), Marty Keanes, Calacone/Moreno, McNary's, Maxies.

Emery's Grocery. Northeast corner of 600 3rd Ave and 5th St. Back side of store faced the canal.

Emery's Grocery. 2nd Ave and 3rd St. Port Schuyler. Edward Emory originally started his business here on May 1, 1885.

Another view of Edward Emery's Grocery. Advertising on the sides of buildings was common place in the 19th and 20th centuries. Jared Bell is credited with designing the first billboards in the 1830s for circus acts like Barnum and Bailey. In the 1860s, businesses bought outdoor space and advertisers began taking advantage of new laws and regs.

Emery's Grocery. Interior. Bond cake and bread were popular staples, introduced in 1915 by the General Baking Co., a large NYC baking conglomerate that was formed in 1911 by merging 21 baking companies in 12 states from the MidAtlantic, Northeast and Midwest.

Star Grocery, 2312 4th Ave, circa 1950. Owner Ben Dinino standing in the doorway. His equipment is displayed at the Watervliet Museum including his scale, sausage making machine, cash register, paper wrapper and slicer. He had a tunnel from the store to his home next door at 2310 4th Ave to transfer daily earnings. Better to be safe than sorry.

Kingsley's Bakery in 1933 was at 16th Street near Broadway. Herbert Kingsley seen driving. His father Walton had a bakery on 16th St where McDonalds' is now.

Side and front photos of J. H. Paulus Pharmacy on the corner of 16th St and 2nd Ave. There were several pharmacies in the city. The building is no longer standing. From the bottom photo it looks like it is leaning.

Paulus Pharmacy interior. Joseph H. Paulus. His funeral was held on April 1, 1919 from his residence on Broadway and at St. Patrick's Church. He died March 30 at his home at 1821 Broadway. His death was a "stroke of "appoplexy" suffered Friday evening." He was 61 years old and had been in the city for the past 11 years and was a popular druggist.

West Troy Railroad Station built in the 1880s between 19th and 23rd Streets Demolished in 1962. Located in the vicinity of Bob's Diner & parking lot.

The West Troy and Green Island Railroad Company was incorporated on October 15, 1870. It was a two mile track connecting the two villages. It connected to the Albany line on one side on the South and Saratoga line on the north Original incorporators were all from Troy: George H. Cramer, Joseph M. Warren, John A. Griswold, William Howard Hart, George B. Warren, Walter P. Warren, Isaac V. Baker, Le Grand Cramer, H. S. Marcy, H. C. Lockwood, John B. Gale, Geo. Parish Ogden and C. L. Alden. The D&H operated the railroad.

Notice the trolley tracks on 19th St crossing the railroad tracks.

A couple of views of Watervliet's train station. In 1958 the station was used by many Troy residents to go to work in Albany. On Feb 14, 1958 the city administration opposed the D&H who wanted to stop selling tickets and was thinking about tearing it down or resuse it. Eight trains stopped daily: five northbound and three southbound.

ALBANY NORTHERN RAILROAD.

PASSENGER ROUTE

BETWEEN

NEW-YORK & MONTREAL

AND INTERMEDIATE PLACES,

VIA

Albany, Saratoga Springs & Lake Champlain

FARE $3 LESS THAN BY ANY OTHER ROUTE.

1856. 1856.

SUMMER ARRANGEMENTS.

TRAINS LEAVE ALBANY

Corner Maiden Lane and Dean Streets, adjoining New-York Central and Hudson River Railroad Depots, connecting with Hudson River Steamers and Railroads for Montreal, Ogdensburgh, and all points North.

7.00 A. M. EXPRESS to Saratoga and Ports on Lake Champlain and Montreal.

10.45 A. M. ACCOMMODATION, to Saratoga only.

5.30 P. M. EXPRESS to Saratoga and Ports on Lake Champlain and Montreal.

☞ BERTHS FREE ON LAKE STEAMERS! ☜

FARE FROM NEW-YORK

Via ALBANY STEAMERS, to

Bprlington,	$4 63
Plattsburgh,	5 38
Montreal,	7 63
Ogdensburgh,	7 38
Whitehall Lake,	3 45
Saratoga,	2 12

From Albany, Fare One Dollar Less.

The equipments of this Road are new and the Track is laid with heavy continuous rail.

Baggage Waggons and Passenger Agents will always be in readiness to convey Baggage to and from Cars and Morning Steamers, Free of Charge.

Tickets can be procured and Baggage Checked on board the Albany Steamers.

N. B. No Sunday Trains Run on this Road.

NEW-YORK, June, 1856.

E. H. DE WITT, Supt.

Passengers on the Albany Northern Railroad would receive free transport on an "omnibus" from the Troy House and the Mansion House in Troy to the Watervliet landing for the day boat to New York City, and all points in between on the Hudson. The landing was at the foot of 16th or 23rd Streets. This is also where the ferries landed.

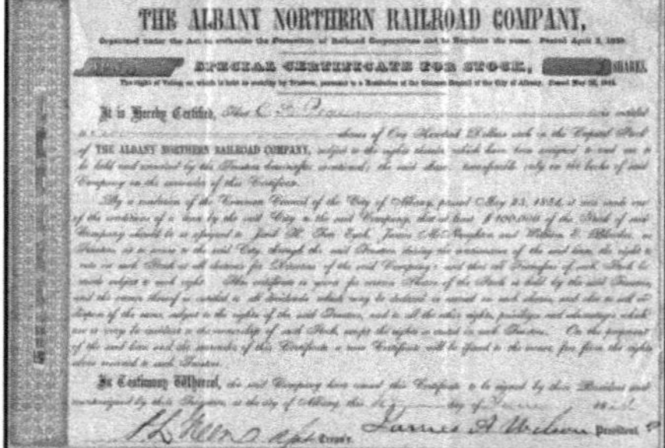

THE ALBANY NORTHERN RAILROAD COMPANY,

SPECIAL CERTIFICATE FOR STOCK, SHARES.

It is Hereby Certified,

of THE ALBANY NORTHERN RAILROAD COMPANY,

23rd street just above RR tracks. Daisy and Ollie's Corner Store on corner and train station just barely visible. Across the tracks for years was Cocca's Diner at 1939 19th St.

Two sisters owned Daisy and Ollie's Corner Store. Also known as Daisy and Ollie's Card Shop (1966). 914 23rd St. They advertised "Carrying Magazines, Books, and Infant's Ware." One was married and the other divorced. Shirley Czarnecki (1926-2018) worked there. There is a cute story about the store in Valerie Falzo's book *Extraordinary Souls I Have Known*. 2020, Covenant Books.

Ironically Daisy & Ollie is a British Children's animated series for preschoolers that started in 2017.

Strand Theater on 374 3rd Ave in Port Schuyler. On Friday, February 13, 1942, nearly 300 children and parents fled for safety when the theater caught on fire. It had just reopened after a two month remodeling job. A roll of film in the projector caught on fire and slightly burned the face and singed the hair of James Purcell, the projectionist. Originally called "Christie's Strand Theater," it was one of the first neighborhood theaters in America. Ironically the movie being shown was "You"ll Never Get Rich." This 1941 musical comedy starred Fed Astaire, Rita Hayworth, Robert Benchely, Cliff Nazarro, with music and lyrics by Cole Porter. The title came from the old Army Song with the lyrics *"You'll never get rich/by digging a ditch/you're in the Army now."* It was Hayworth's first starring role in a big budgeted Columbia Pictures production. It made her a star and helped revive Astaire's career after he broke ranks with Ginger Rogers. Ironically the movie was about a theater owner and womanizer (Benchley) who enlists the aid of his manager Robert Curtis (Astaire) to woo dancer Shelia Winthrop (Hayworth). One of the film's songs, *Since I Kissed My Baby Goodbye,* was nominated for an Academy Award for Best Song. The Strand had 305 seats.

Family Theater (originally the Sans Souci) and Rowell's Grocery store on the right. c. 1914. 16th street between broadway and 2nd Ave, south side. The Sans Souci was called "The Strand of Watervliet" in 1916. It had 400 seats. On November 10, 1910 the Republicans held a mass meeting at the theater discussing national and local issues. The Family Theater was operating prior to 1931 but closed by 1950. In 1946 Samuel Rosenblatt, who owned the Strand Theater took over the lease on the Family Theater.

Milton Rowell Meat Market was next to the Sans Souci (Family) Theater. It was destroyed by fired in 1916.

Grand Theater at 2431-39 3rd Ave between 24th and 25th street. Opened prior to 1926. It had 380 seats. Had Vaudeville in the 1920s and an Amateur night in 1929. Was being sold as a warehouse in 1967. Besides the Grand, Sans Souci and Strand, there was the Empire, Hudson and Star Theater (Broadway). On Nov. 3 & 7, 1923, Billy Roy presented his Vaudville act "Joy of Childhood."

John C. Covert Manufacturing Company. Began in Troy in 1873. Moved to West Troy in 1879, SW corner of 16th St and 5th Ave. Incorporated in Watervliet in January, 1900. Made saddlery, harness and wrought iron chains, harness snaps, breast heel and rein chains. Several buildings were in operation. After several fires, Covert moved to 1801 Avenue A. Made harness snaps, swivel snaps, open-eye bit, chain and trace snaps, snaps and thimbles for horse and cattle ties, adjustable web and rope halters, and rope goods, consisting of rope halters, horse and cattle ties, halter leads, weight and hitching cords, hammock ropes, lariat tethers, picket pins, and also adjustable soldering irons, rod post hitchers and chain goods consisting of breast, halter, rein, post, trace and heel chains, hitching posts, balling irons, safety gate hooks, pant stretchers, wagon jacks, etc. The finishing plant was destroyed by fire on August 29, 1917.

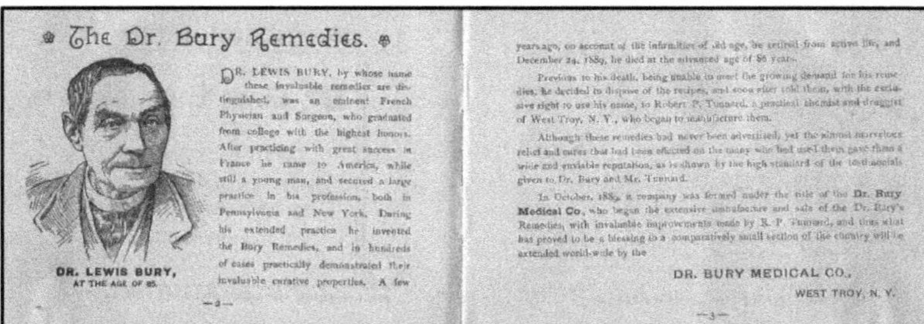

The Dr. Bury Remedies.

DR. LEWIS BURY,
AT THE AGE OF 85.

DR. LEWIS BURY, by whose name these invaluable remedies are distinguished, was an eminent French Physician and Surgeon, who graduated from college with the highest honors. After practicing with great success in France he came to America, while still a young man, and secured a large practice in his profession, both in Pennsylvania and New York. During his extended practice he invented the Bury Remedies, and in hundreds of cases practically demonstrated their invaluable curative properties. A few

—2—

years ago, on account of the infirmities of old age, he retired from active life, and December 24, 1889, he died at the advanced age of 86 years.

Previous to his death, being unable to meet the growing demand for his remedies, he decided to dispose of the recipes, and soon after sold them, with the exclusive right to use his name, to Robert P. Tunnard, a practical chemist and druggist of West Troy, N. Y., who began to manufacture them.

Although these remedies had never been advertised, yet the almost marvelous relief and cures that had been effected on the many who had used them gave them a wide and enviable reputation, as is shown by the high standard of the testimonials given to Dr. Bury and Mr. Tunnard.

In October, 1889, a company was formed under the title of the **Dr. Bury Medical Co.**, who began the extensive manufacture and sale of the Dr. Bury's Remedies, with invaluable improvements made by R. P. Tunnard, and thus what has proved to be a blessing to a comparatively small section of the country will be extended world-wide by the

DR. BURY MEDICAL CO.,
WEST TROY, N. Y.

—3—

Covert also created in 1889 the Dr. Bury Medical Company. Medicines consist of lung balsam, catarrh snuff and camphor ointment. An employee of Covert was Robert. P. Tunnard who had patents in 1886 for "Dr. Burr's Reliable Camphor Ointment," "Dr. Bury's Reliable Lung Balsam," "Dr. Bury's Reliable Catarrh Snuff." Tunnard had been declared a deserter in the Civil War though served honorably. He was elected president of West Troy 1879-1880.

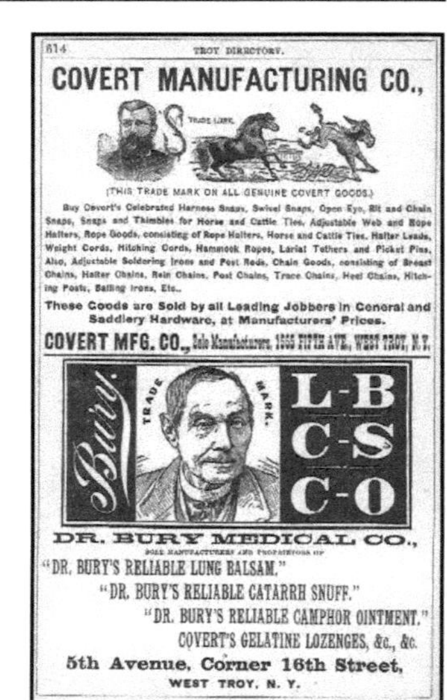

Stebbin's Grocery Store. 734-5th Ave in Port Schuyler. Napoleon Stebbins operated the store from 1935 to 1965. He was a school crossing guard at Third Ave and Seventh St. Johnny and Catherine Gaughan ran the store before him.

United Traction Trolley series 600. United Traction Company was formed in 1899, formerly the Albany Railway.

John Graham Merchant Taylor. 1623 Broadway. Circa early 1900s. Came to West Troy in 1852. Engaged with Abram Myers as clothing cutter, and in 1854, with Gunsalus and Wilks, on Whitehall Street. In 1876, established the custom clothing business in the Lobdell Block, and in 1879 erected the brick building, corner 17th St and Broadway and continuing the business on a larger scale until his death, in August, 1905. Prominent in business circles and was an influential citizen. His son Edward J. Graham, was a graduate of LaSalle Institute, succeeded to the business and consisted of gent's furnishings in connection with custom tailoring. In 1909 eliminated clothing and opened an exclusively haberdasher and gentlemen's furnishings emporium, with a large stock of up-to-date line of good suitable to the demand of buyers of first class wearing apparel, in the latest novelties of the season. "His method of doing business, his popularity, in connection with the fine line of goods always in stock, has enabled him to meet the wants of his patrons, both in quality and price, placing him in the lead in his line of business." In 1839 on the west side of Liberty Street.

23rd Street between 2nd and 3rd avenue on north side circa 1920s. Cobble stone in alley way still exists today.

James Roy & Company 1839-1908, Broadway, Port Schuyler. James Roy went into the woolen manufacture business in 1839. In 1848 Roy changed to the exclusive production of woolen shawls. He also included by 1840 the Roy Butt and Hinge works. By 1860, 40% of the entire woolen shawl production in America came from Roy's. Benjamin Knower became a partner with Roy.

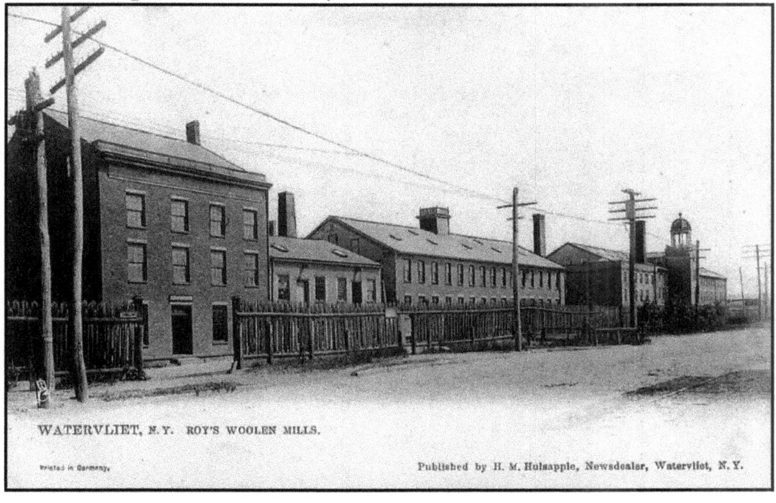

James Roy and Company 1839-1908, Broadway, Port Schuyler. The number of employees for both the woolen shawl and hinge and butt factories totaled 470. The Hooker Venetian Blind Co. took over one of the buildings in 1930 and in the late 1940s Passonno Paint took over the entire complex of buildings. Below: Workers in the Roy Mills, circa 1900.

Walt's Diner (old trolley car). 1556 Broadway. c. 1950s. Opened 1951 by Walter Guyette. Patrolman Al Reed on bike.

Walt's Diner, Broadway. Known also as Walt's Central Diner.

Tilley Ladder Factory and Home in 1887 at 1st Ave and 2nd St. Filed for bankruptcy in 2004 over insurance costs (30% of sales). They made ladders for 149 years with 100 workers.

Original Tilley Ladder Factory, 1st Ave and 2nd St. Manufacturer of ladders and scaffolding from 1855-2004. Photo taken in 1887. Founder John Tilley is standing on the roof. The house to the right was this home.

JOHN TILLEY

Founder and owner of the business from 1855 to 1878

Founder John Tilley (1806-1878). Tilley Ladder Company started as a barrel maker & ladders in Grafton, NY, before moving to West Troy in 1855. His son John S. Tilley took over in 1878 at the 1st Ave and 2nd St shop. A fire in 1915 saw a bigger two story brick factory of 20,000 square feet built between First and Second Streets. They made some 17 different models. Block long factory building is now apartments.

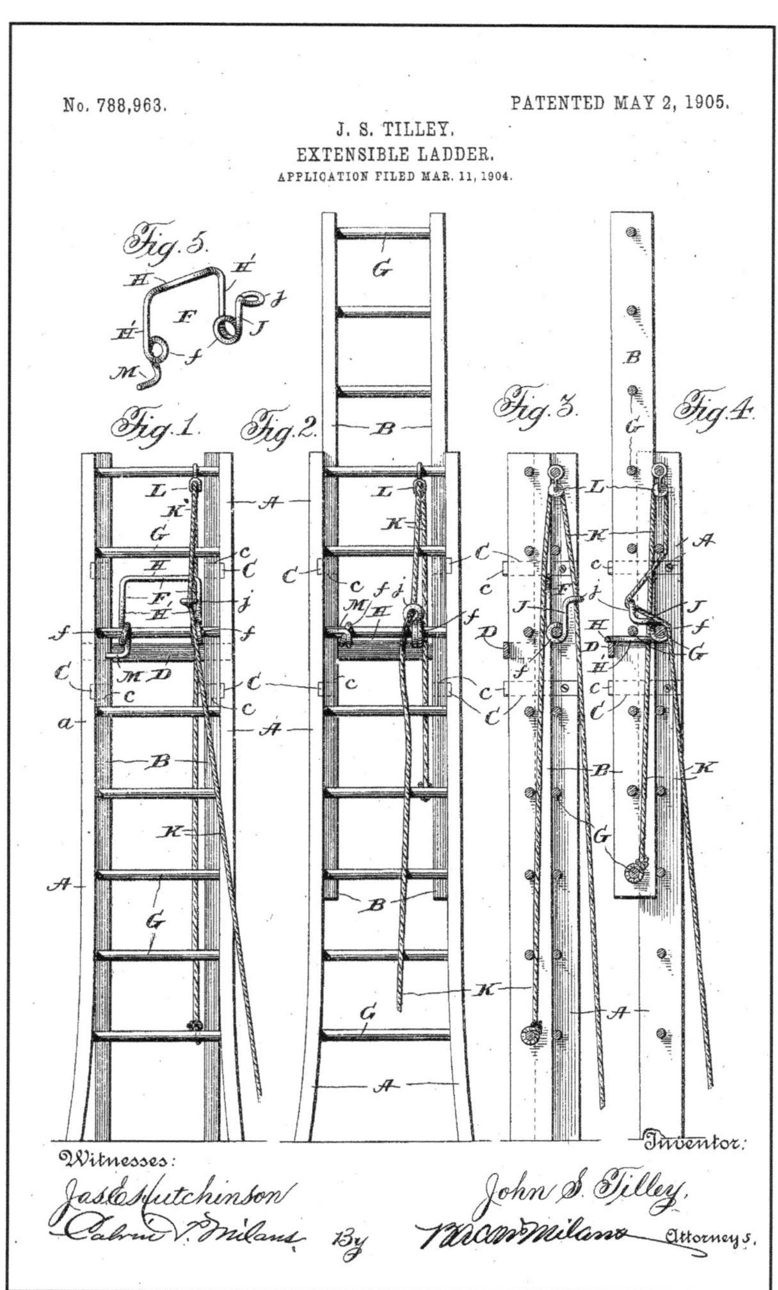

John S. Tilley had six patents on ladders. This extension ladder was patented on May 2, 1905.

John S. Tilley (1852-1913) had six patents on ladders. In 1907 Tilley had doubled its manufacturing capacity due to high demand of ladders, scaffolds, staging, ladder hooks and flag poles Went out of business in 2004 oveer skyrocketing insurance costs.

Tilley Ladder Co. Wagon.

Former Tilley Ladder firm. Now Tilley Apartments, renovated by Redburn Development in 2014 into more than 60 upscale loft-like apartments. Good adapted reuse.

James Tilley, from Grafton; where he established the cooperage business, head linings, together with coopers tools, and as a side line manufacture ladders; his son, James Tilley, being connected with him in the ladder part of the business; came to West Troy in 1850; James was connected with the business until 1865; withdrew when the firm of Tilley & Littlefield established the ice business; dissolved later; James went to New York where he died in 1906.

J. S. Tilley bought his father's interest in the business in 1864, and with his brother formed the co-partnership of J. S. Tilley & Company, continuing until 1873, when it became J. S. Tilley; the present proprietor of the largest plant of like character in this section; the works and yards are on a large area on First and Second Streets and the stock of adjustable ladders of all kinds and scaffolding is large and the material of the best quality; a specialty is made of flag poles of any size; one of the features of the firm are some fine specimens on exhibit at all times; with up-to-date machinery, and the employment of expert mechanics he is able to meet all contracts in quality, workmanship and delivery; the clerical work of the business is looked after by his efficient bookkeeper, Miss Rose Leach and Miss Nina Martin, stenographer, office No. 122 Second Street.

— History of the City of Watervliet, N.Y. 1630-1910.

Broadway & 15th Street. Now the area of the Senior Center.

James Wager purchased an old stoneware building and added another in the 1870s and created a foundry for making cast iron stoves. About 1800 Daniel E. Paris bought it and created the West Side Foundry makers of cast iron stoves. In 1894, William, William N. and Charles Sleicher took over. Discontinued stoves in 1900, switched to general casting and architectural ironwork. Second Ave and 26th St.

19th street and 2nd avenue. Now Walgreens Pharmacy. Notice Mooradian's furniture store and Joe Delollo"s Liquor store in picture.

Sam's Food Market , 25th St, 1972.

School #8. 4th Ave between 23rd and 24th Sts. 1967.

Reflections East Disco. Located on Broadway at the foot of the old Congress Street Bridge. 1979. Former site of Jolly Chef restaurant and also a Mike's Sub, jewelry store, barber shop, etc. It was the first and only Disco in the city and became notorious in its later years. It was owned in the 80s and 90s by Jack Buchman who later became a stock trader. His father owned Barclay Home Products in Cohoes. Jack died in 2009 at age 66.

Conroy's Soda Shop, 711 19th street.

Old Watervliet Mall. Price Chopper and Fays. Price Chopper decided to build bigger and destroyed St. Patrick's Church (originally established in 1840 in West Troy) for Catholics. Later a new church built on land of two square blocks on 19th St between 5th and 6th Aves. It was designed based on the Upper Basilica at Lourdes France. A huge Meneely Bell nearly 10,000 pounds rang on Easter Sunday, 1907. Closed in 2012. Leveled in 2013 by Price Chopper among controversy. The bell is saved at the Watervliet Historical Society.

Houses on 23rd street between 8th and 9th avenue. 1989.

Swichman's Grill. 2300 2nd Ave. Destroyed for Daniel P. Quinn Apartments. Senior housing.

Looking north on Broadway from north end of Arsenal, 1950s.

Bob's Diner, 929 19th St. 1986. 24 hour service to this day. Owned by the family for over 41 years. This family friendly diner has been serving locals since Bob Ziter opened on August 9, 1979. Originally it was called Verni's Diner. A good place to eat at three in the morning.

Gardners Grocery Store at 402 16th St. Cast Iron store front probably made by Jame McKinney Iron Founders in Albany.

Trolley track on 19th Street. Trolleys disappeared shortly after World War II in the Capital District.

Mid State Kitchens. Facing south on Broadway at 16th St (Sherlock's on the right). The point Broadway continued on the left (east) side of building and 1st Ave started on the right (west) side of building. The beginning of 1st Ave!

Keane's News Room. Marty Keane, owner, circa 1950. 701 3rd avenue..

Alpine Lunch and Grill, 1839 2nd Ave. 1978. Chris Huban owned it in the 1960s-70s as a country western style bar. Later OTB in the 1980s. Originally Watervliet Diner from 1897 to 1933 at 1897 2nd Ave then became Miss Watervliet Diner until 1944. In 1945 moved to 1825 2nd Ave, then the following year moved to 1839 2nd Ave where it currently sits. It became the Alpine in 1961 and lasted until about 1978. It is believed to be a Bixler Diner. They made diners from 1931 to 1937 and were known for their wide swath.The diners were known by their two wide double hung windows and barrel roof with a fancy profile at the ends. There are a few still in operation in New York State.

Ad on left is from Dec 7, 1973.

Sid Schillinger's Bar and Grill, 1301 7th Ave, circa 1950. Located in the Temperance Hill section. Popular before and after WWII. Also known as the Lucky 13 after that.

Schuyler Pub, 2nd St & 2nd Ave. In the early AM of Aug 23, 1983 the Schanz Beverage Center was robbed of 13 cases of Molson's beer. The crook called the Pub's owner Charles Burmaster to try and sell him the beer. Didn't work.

1st Ave between 15th and 16th Streets. View down the street. Notice the Belgian Blocks lining the street. Many blocks still survive under the modern day asphalt.

23rd St looking west. Freihofer Bakery wagon. Freihofer opened in Lansingburgh on March 12, 1913 and this scene was commonplace until 1962. Sold out in 1987 to General Foods.

Looking north on Broadway. August 14, 1973. Entire block gone.

Broadway looking south from 16th street, July 13, 1962. Before the wrecking ball.

Another view looking north on Broadway between 15th and 16th street. April 27, 1973.

A&P (The Great Atlantic & Pacific Tea Company) on 19th street. Early food chain from 1859-2015. From 1915-75 largest grocery store in America. An icon of the day, you could grind your own fresh coffee beans. In the 1940s captured 10% of all grocery spending. A major competitor was Grand Union which operated mostly in the Northeast.

Watervliet Post Office, Broadway. The first post office was located at the corner of River and Ferry Streets (Broadway and 14th St) in 1816. Abijah Wheeler was postmaster.

Next Page. FIRE STATIONS. The first fire engine, Old Niagara #1 was commissioned in 1829. The old fire departments had three hand engines and two hook and ladder companies including The Rip Van Winkle Engine Co #1, Protection Engine Co #2, and Conqueror Engine Co #3, Hercules Hook and Ladder Co #1 and Spartan Hook and Ladder #2. In 1864 the first steam fire engine companies were organized: James Roy #1, James Duffy #2 and Martin Tierney #3. These steamers were in service until 1878 when a public water works system was introduced. The village then had four hose companies and one Hook and Ladder Co: Oswald Hose Co #1, 1859; Michael Kelly Hose Co #2, 1870; Thomas McIntyre Co #3, 1873; Protective Hose Co #4, 1878, and S. J. Gleason Hook and Ladder Co #1, 1872. Gleason/Oswald were on the same site on Broadway. Served as the last fire station until 1969 at the east side of Broadway north of 15th St when the new station was built on the south side of 13th St between 1st and 2nd Ave. Three buildings still stand: McIntyre in Port Schuyler, Protective Hose on 23rd St and Michael Kelly on 21st St.

Protection Hose Company #4. 610 23rd street. The building is still standing but converted to a two family residence.

Fire House 23rd St, 1884. West Troy #4 is still on the building at 610 23rd St.

McIntyre Hose Company #3. Port Schuyler . Circa early 1900.

McIntyre's Hose Company.

McIntyre's Fire House. Walter A. Jones Post Fife & Drums Corps.

Michael Kelly Hose Company located at 30 21st street. This station closed by 1930. It is now the site of Parker Bros Memorial Garage. Circa early 1900s. The Hose Company was organized in 1870 with Michael Kelly as the chief.

S. J. Gleason Hook and Ladder Company, 1560 Broadway, 1860.

Watervliet Firehouse Headquarters on Broadway until 1969.

Watervliet Firetruck

Watervliet Fire Department - Engine #5

Watervliet Arsenal Fire Department 1918. The Arsenal Fire Department responded to many fires in the area.

First Baptist Church Fire. Corner of 16th St and 3rd Ave.

Buffalo Row Fire. This row of houses were located across from City Hall. 15th St was known as Buffalo Street until the 1880s. Thus they were called the Buffalo Row. Note the former Dutch Church in the background.

Meneely Mansion Fire on 1st Ave. April 2, 1974.

Fire near City Hall.

Early Fire Truck (wagon).

Oswald Hose Company #1 of West Troy (Watervliet) 1885. Located at the same site as the Gleason Hook and Ladder had been. Both were at 1558-1560 Broadway.

James Duffy Steamer #2 ,West Troy Fire Wagon, circa late 1800s.

The Matton Shipyards

If you visit Peeble's Island State Park in Van Schaick Island/Waterford you will drive by a series of buildings with the name Matton on it. Famous for making tugboats and canal boats it really started in Watervliet. According to an excellent article on the subject found in the Cohoes Spindle City Historic Society newsletter, Volume 14, No 1, Spring 2011, states:

"John E. Matton's name first appeared in the Troy/Cohoes/Waterford City Directory in 1902, when he was listed as a ship carpenter living at 30 Middle Street in Waterford, but the firm he established was dated as beginning in 1900. In 1903 Matton moved to Hudson River Road, where he remained until 1925 when he moved to 849 Second Avenue in Lansingburgh. Matton's first business listing appeared in the directory in 1910 as John E. Matton, Waterford Dry-Dock, Lock 6, Champlain Canal. His advertisement stated: "Boats built, repaired and thoroughly overhauled, Custom Sawing and Planing Mill, phone 525." Lock 6 of the original Champlain Canal was located just north of Waterford."

John Matton's father, P. Jesse Matton, owned the Watervliet Dry-Dock and Boat Yard in 1913 but had previously maintained a drydock on the Erie Canal south of Thirteenth Street in Watervliet. He remained in business during WWI and died in 1923.

Peter Jesse Matton owned the Watervliet Dry-Dock and Boat Yard in 1913. He previously maintained a drydock on the Erie Canal south of 13th St in Watervliet. He moved to 1285 First Avenue in Lansingburgh in 1909 but still maintained his business in Watervliet. He was married to Minnie Eda Trembley Van Vranken, her second husband. Peter's father was also Peter J. which is why he went by P. Jesse Matton in business. In 1919 he was elected VP of the Watervliet "Ghost Club." That year he built four 800-ton barges, the biggest of its kind ever built in the city being two feet deeper than the usual barge size. He remained in business during WWI. He was sued in 1921 for not building a boat by Lewis Martin of New York City. He was forced to go bankrupt in June 1921 and died two years later on Oct 1, 1923. He was killed in an automobile accident on Glens Falls-Saratoga Road near Ganesvoort in Saratoga Springs. The Ghost Club asked NYS to investigate the dangerous curve where he died. He is buried in Albany Rural Cemetery.

22 TROY [1919] DIRECTORY

P. JESSE MATTON

Proprietor of

The Watervliet Dry Dock and Ship Yard

First Class Canal Boats and Barges of any model or style built at lowest possible figures. Repairing and thorough overhauling. Tugs, Yachts and Contract Work a Specialty. Plant equipped with the most modern air tools and other machinery. Modern House Building and Repairing.

PHONE 499

DRY DOCKS AT FIRST AVENUE AND TWELFTH STREET
SHIP YARD: NINTH AND BROADWAY
WATERVLIET, NEW YORK

D&H Caboose #359592 taken on July, 1977.

Garnet AC Softball Champions 1939.

Queenies Tavern. Near the Grand Theater on 3rd Ave and 25th St.

Inside of Queenies. Notice the Wurlitzer jukebox on the left.

Looking north on Broadway from north end of Arsenal, 1950s.

Broadway Sunoco Station. Near present City Hall.

Collins House. 16th St and Broadway. Originally the West Troy Exchange. A hotel on this site was leased by Ebenezer Powell in 1831 and called the Mansion House. In 1838 a building was rebuilt by H. N. Carr and leased to Mrs. Cloe Manchester Powell. She named it the West Troy Exchange until 1844. It became the Collins House in 1866 when Isaac Collins bought it.

Collins House. One of seven hotels and boarding houses during the hayday of the Erie Canal. It was opposite of the current McDonalds. circa 1890s.

One hundred forty years ago the South Reformed Church (Jermain Church) on December 30,1874 was dedicated into service. Invocation was offered by Reverend A. Dickson. Here is a photo of the laying of the cornerstone on September 22, 1872. (Photo courtesy of Robert Collier)

James Strates Show, Schuyler Flats, circa 1950. For years people looked forward to the Carnaval on the southern limits of the city.

In 1923 James E. Strates, a Greek immigrant, began his first show. He came to America in 1909 and, like many immigrants, worked at a number of odd jobs. In 1919, he joined a carnival athletic show as a wrestler taking on all challengers. In 1923, he acquired Southern Tier Shows and in 1932 changed its name to James E. Strates Shows. He continued to build and manage the carnival until his death in 1959. The author tried to runaway with the show, age 10.

After the death of James E. Strates, his son, assumed responsibility for the carnival and still operates it today. James Strates was an innovator from the beginning, bringing many firsts to the amusement business such as cooperative promotions, advance ticket sales and a centralized ticket system.

James E. Strates Shows' carnival midway was founded by a young Greek immigrant, James E. Strates, best known in the early days as "Young Strangler Lewis." While working at a shoe factory, cotton mill, restaurant and other jobs, he perfected his skill as a wrestler and turned professional. Under the name of "Young Strangler Lewis," he grappled on a circuit from Buffalo to Philadelphia and from Boston to Syracuse.

Lewis and Bozinis joined Lee Schaefer's Athletic Show which was part of the World at Home Shows, a traveling carnival. Both men traveled on the New York circuit during the winter and with the show during the summer. By the end of 1919, Lewis was one of the top contenders for the world middleweight championship and one of the top mat promoters of his time.

In 1924 James E. Strates bought out his partners. He continued to wrestle into the 1930s while promoting matches and managing his friend, Nick Bozinis, for a short time.

In 1920 Young Strangler Lewis received his title shot against Joe Turner, Middleweight Champion of the World. The older, more experienced Turner won after one hour, 32 minutes and 11 seconds. In 1922 Lewis and partners Bozinis and W. L. Platt reassembled the show and named it Southern Tier Shows, from upstate New York. In 1923, its first season, the show consisted of a three-abreast merry-go-round by Allan Herschell, a Ferris wheel by Eli Bridge, an athletic show, 15 concessions, three side shows and five hard-rubber-tire trucks. It took 24 hours to move the show 22 miles from Bath, N.Y. to its first stop in Wayland, N.Y.

FIRST CHURCH BUILDING IN WEST TROY, N. Y.

Dedicated July 10, 1816, and first site of the South Reformed Church, occupied by them for 30 years, abandoned 1874. View shows also first Chapel and Parsonage.

In July 10, 1816, the South Reformed Church moved into the building showed above which was located at 959 Broadway.

The South Reformed Protestant Dutch Church of Washington and Gibbonsville was formed on March 22, 1814. They met in the old school house on the corner of Second Avenue and Sixth Street which had been a gift to the village from the Van Renesselaer Family. This building later became the home of the Thomas B. Flynn American Legion Post # 1035.

Reformed Church of Washington and Gibbonsville
Erected 1814-1816

SOUTH REFORMED CHURCH,
WEST TROY, N. Y.
"Memorial Building" erected by James B. Jermain, 1874.

Jermain Memorial Presbyterian Church was built in 1872 for the South Reformed Church. James Barclay Jermain, a rich lawyer and businessness man paid for the erection of this church in the village of Port Schuyler. It was named for his father Silvanus P. Jermain. Below location of the Watervliet Historical Society in the old Dutch church.

Interior

Exterior

Malta Temple

Hospitallers, also spelled Hospitalers, also called Order of Malta or Knights of Malta, formally (since 1961) Sovereign Military and Hospitaller Order of St. John of Jerusalem, of Rhodes, and of Malta, previously (1113–1309) Hospitallers of St. John of Jerusalem, (1309–1522); Order of the Knights of Rhodes, (1530–1798); Sovereign and Military Order of the Knights of Malta, or (1834–1961) Knights Hospitaller of St. John of Jerusalem; a religious military order that was founded at Jerusalem in the 11th century and that, headquartered in Rome, continues its humanitarian tasks in most parts of the modern world under several slightly different names and jurisdictions.

French Catholic Church.
On 6th Ave.

Trinity Episcopal Church.
1330 First Ave.

Ashline Moving Company. A fleet of trucks ready to move. Still in business at 632 3rd Ave., the original location.

Ashline Moving Company. Still in business. Originally started out as the Old Saratoga Transfer & Warehouse in 1918 by Alfred and Margaret Ashline. In 1954 created the tag line "When you Make Your Next Move." One of America's oldest moving companies.

Ashline Moving Company. Ice and coal. Looks like they also moved ice and coal with attractive women on the truck using either as an advertising gimmick or fan.

James D. Hayes Esso Gas Station. Operated Esso (Exxon) stations starting in 1938 on 19th St. Took over the station at 19th and Second Ave in 1942 and ran until the new Congress St bridge was built. Around 1970 took over the Exxon station on 13th and Broadway until I-787 was built. Died in 2003 at age 91. Obituary at https://www.legacy.com/us/obituaries/timesunion-albany/name/james-hayes-obituary?id=4892116

Raising the flag on the Children's Play Ground, Watervliet, N. Y.

April 27, 1893. Up for inspection: N. F. JONES, W. Brainard, 346 E. 20th Street. Tug CORA, of Albany, with a 12 x 13 engine was on the East River Saturday. Purchased by R. W. Mathews of Philadelphia for Cuban parties. Two tugs were ready for launching at New Baltimore on Saturday. One, 60 x 14' with a 14 x 18" high-pressure engine is for Charles Lodge of West Troy. The other, powered by an 16 x 18" engine is for Ward & Pratt, also of West Troy.

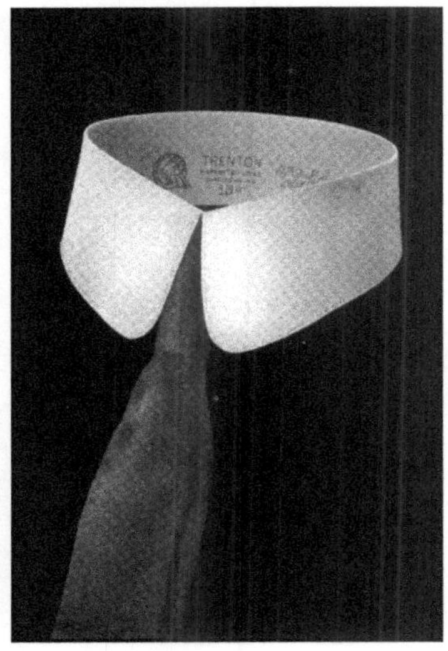

William Barker Company-Constructed in 1899 and located at 1534 Broadway opposite the old Post Office. Manufacturer of linen "Barker" brand collars and shirts. While they made them in Watervliet they used a Troy address since Troy was famous as the "Collar City." They had offices on the West Coast as well. In 1902, William Barker, Jr., went to Congress protesting the bill that would create the 8 hour work week.

Homes on east side of Broadway removed for I-787. Just below 13th Street looking north. 1960s. Jim Hayes Esso Gas Station on Broadway.

Corner of 16th St & Broadway.

Hiltons Grocery horse and wagon. 1417 Broadway. John Thomas Connell is the man standing by the wagon.

O'Brien Ice House. 7th street and Broadway. One of the busiest ice houses in the area. Ice harvesting was a major industry until the refrigerator was invented in the 1920s. Held about 1500 tons of ice. Burned on Aug 8, 1904.

Fairview Humane Home. The C.L. Mather home was purchased in 1888 by the Albany Society for the Prevention of Cruelty to Children for an orphanage. Fairview was absorbed by the Troy Orphan Asylum July 31, 1956.

Trojan ICE CREAM
Trojan ICE CREAM

DiNuzzo's Grocery and family.

CRUDO'S
Parched

Above: Unknown family. Below: Corpus Christi Day, 23rd Street and 2nd Avenue. 1935.

Class at West Troy School 2.

Knights of Columbus. 18th street and 2nd Ave. Moved into the former Walton Motors after I-787 construction from 1464 Broadway.

Family Market 1399 Broadway.

Gus's Hot Dog. 212 25th St. This is the 1954 picture of the interior on opening day. Still serving mini hot dogs with special sauce and hamburgers to this day. A must stop for the hungry. Started by Gus Haita and now run by his son Steve. The author often has four dogs with the works and a Greek Burger with two chocalate milks. A must stop.

Three bridges crossed the river from Troy to Watervliet. The first in 1874 was a toll bridge. The second was built in 1915-17 and was a toll bridge until May 24, 1920. The third and present bridge was built in 1971 for access to I-787 but ends on Ferry Street not Congress. Originally the bridge area served as a park (below) and watching the bridge open for steamboats to pass was a common attraction.

The Congress Street Bridge pre-1913.

Original Parker Bros Funeral Home, 2013 Broadway. William F. and Joseph Parker (Brothers) established the funeral business in 1881.William was the leader of the Watervliet Democratic party for years and held many meetings, political and other wise at the morgue.

Jerry Meyer's Atlantic Gas Station at 3010 19th Street east of 12th Ave on May 14, 1957.

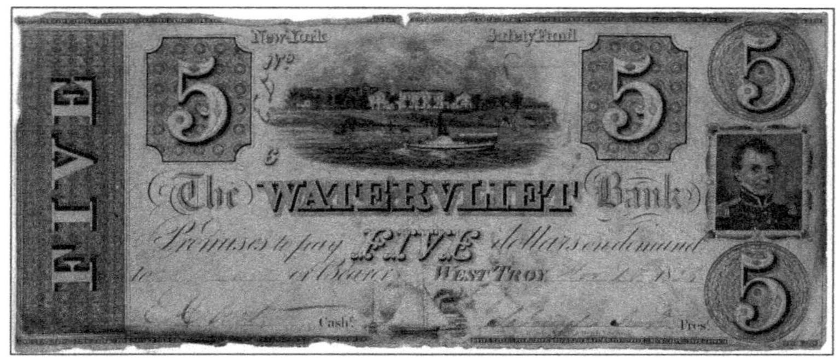

Five dollar bank note from the Watervliet Bank in West Troy in 1836. The bank was incorporated in 1836. Location in the Watervliet House, southwest corner River and Buffalo Streets (Broadway and 15th). President, J. C. Schuyler; vice-president, Edward Learned; cashier, Egbert Olcott; teller, Everett T. Witbeck; clerk, George W. Wheeler. Failed 1841. The panic of 1837 was the cause.

Watervliet Pharmacy, 601 19th St and 6th Ave. Enlarged and remodeled in Nov. 1956.

Watervliet Iron and Brass Foundry, 1946. Was on Cohoes Road. Went out of business in February, 1989.

Entering Watervliet from the Congress St Bridge. 1940s.

St. Coleman's Home, 11 Hawell Rd. Originally St. Coleman's Orphans Asylum, an orphanage, but now serves autistic and emotionally challenged children.

Third Ave above 25th St. On Feb 26, 1900 three buildings burned. Founded in 1850 by William Knight and George Harrison. Originally was on the East side of 14th, between Congress and Christie Streets. Specialized in agricultural castings and screw wrenches. Occupied 14 city lots. Building and land was for sale in 1936. Really was located in Colonie.

Pat Kelley's Restaurant and Livery Stable. 38 River St. (located in Washington) now Broadway.

One of seven hotels in West Troy (became Watervliet in 1896) during the hay days of the Erie Canal. The Acheson Block Building first built as a hotel in 1875 at 19th Street and 3rd Avenue.

A. DeLollo Grocery and Confectionery Store. 701 19th St. corner 7th Ave.

DeLollo Grocery Store. Interior.

De Lollo "American Italian" Grocer y Store. Exterior.

William H. Conroy. 19th St and 7th Ave. Young woman with braids.

Birds Grocery. 717 19th Street.

WGY Food Store. Local radio station WGY produced a small chain of grocery stores that opened in the 1920s. At one time thee were over 130 independently owned stores mostly along the Mohawk Valley and within 75 miles of Schenectady. Still in business in the 1960s.

Old Broadway on the East side, southeast of the Arsenal. House on far left is number 968. Area demolished for I-787.

Dyke Cigars. Tom Dyke started it. His cigars were sold throughout New York State. John B. Dyke, VP died in 1952.

15th and Broadway looking west, circa 1950s.

Merlin J. Zeh. MD, 92 at his death in 1959 of 1825 Third Ave., Watervliet. Was a physician for 70 years. Born in Knox, he received his medical degree from Union University, Albany Medical College, in 1889. He was the 305th licensed pharmacist in this state. He became a qualified medical doctor at the age of 21. The medical course was three years then but he qualified in two, because of his pharmacy training and his grades at Albany Medical College. In 1953, Dr. Zeh was honored by Watervliet residents as one of the oldest practitioners in the United States.

15th St and Broadway looking east. Home on upper right hand corner was known as the Rock House and was the original home of James Gibbon, the founder of Gibbonsville (1803-1836).

Photo of 3rd Ave going into Broadway below 8th St in the 1950s.

Broadway and 15th street looking south. The Masonic Temple on the right and Police Station on the right. All buildings on the left destroyed for I-787.

Looking north on Broadway.

City Hall and Fire House.

Broadway and 19th St. 1965. Buildings are gone.

A Meneely Bell ready for installation.

The Meneely Bell Foundry was established in 1826 by Andrew Meneely, upon the present location of this foundry. Mr. Meneely learned the trade of a brass founder and mathematical instrument maker of Mr. Julius Hanks, who kept a small shop or foundry, which was then located on the west side of Broadway, about one hundred feet south of Buffalo street, in what was then called the village of Gibbonsville. Mr. Meneely commenced business as a manufacturer of civil engineering instruments, and also the manufacturing of church bells and town clocks. This business steadily increased, and in 1835 he took Jonas V. Oothout into partnership with him, the firm name being Meneely & Oothout. This firm continued to exist until 1841, when Mr. Oothout withdrew, and Mr. Meneely continued the business alone until 1849, when he took his son Edwin A. in the business as a partner, the firm name being Andrew Meneely & Son. In 1851 Andrew Meneely died, and this business was thereafter conducted by his two sons, Edwin A. and George R., under the firm name of Andrew Meneely's Sons; and a few years thereafter changed to E. A. & G. R. Meneely. Soon after the decease of Mr. Andrew Meneely, his successors discontinued the manufacture of civil engineering instruments (Mr. Meneely having discontinued the manufacture of town clocks previous to his decease), and gave their exclusive attention to the manufacture of church bells and chimes of bells, fire-alarm bells, etc. In 1874 Mr. George R. Meneely withdrew from this business, and thereafter the present firm name of Meneely & Co. was adopted, the present members of the firm being Edwin A. Meneely and his sons, Andrew H. and George K. This foundry has a world-wide reputation, having for many years sent bells of its manufacture to all parts of the world. The proprietors of this foundry have from time to time made several improvements in the form of the bells and the manner of hanging them, so as to make the labor of ringing as easy as possible.

Meneely Bell Foundry and Post Office on the West side of Broadway between 15th and 16th streets.

The first Meneely bell foundry was established in 1826 in West Troy by Andrew Meneely, a former apprentice in the foundry of Benjamin Hanks. Two of Andrew's sons continued to operate the foundry after his death, and it remained a family operation until its closure. Andrew and his Brother Clinton were rivals and even sued each other. They could look across the river and see each other's buildings. Both closed in 1952. There are thousands of Meneely bells still ringing around the world. One of the largest ever cast is in the possession of the Watervliet Historical Society.

Whitbeck Ferry coming through the Side Cut.

On March 6, 1898, a freshet caused the approaches to the Troy and West Troy Ferry and the 23rd St Ferry to rise. The 23rd St. Ferry started making trips again after several weeks of not being in operation.

Ferry, city of Watervliet.

West Troy Ferry. Before The construction of the Congress Street bridge in the 1870s there were Ferry's between Troy and West Troy at 14th , 16th and 23rd sts. 16th street was originally known as ferry street.

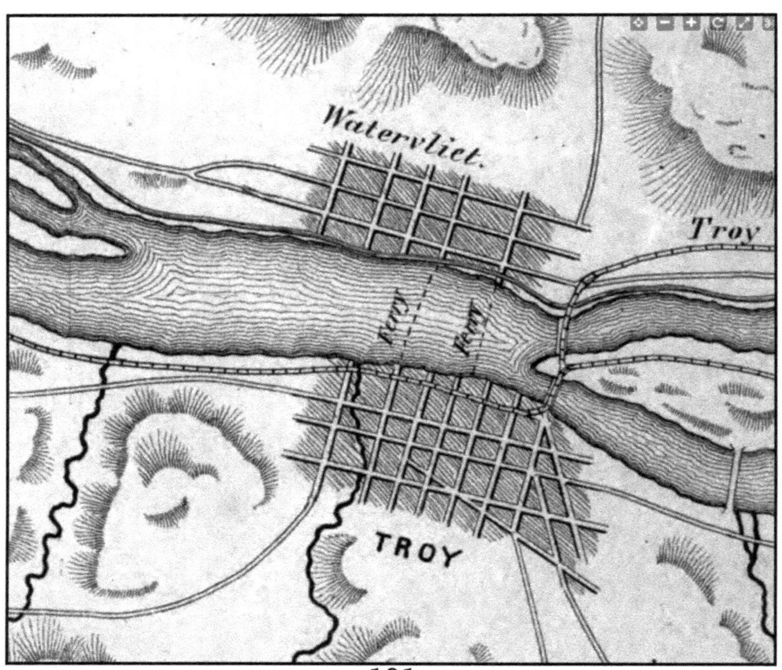

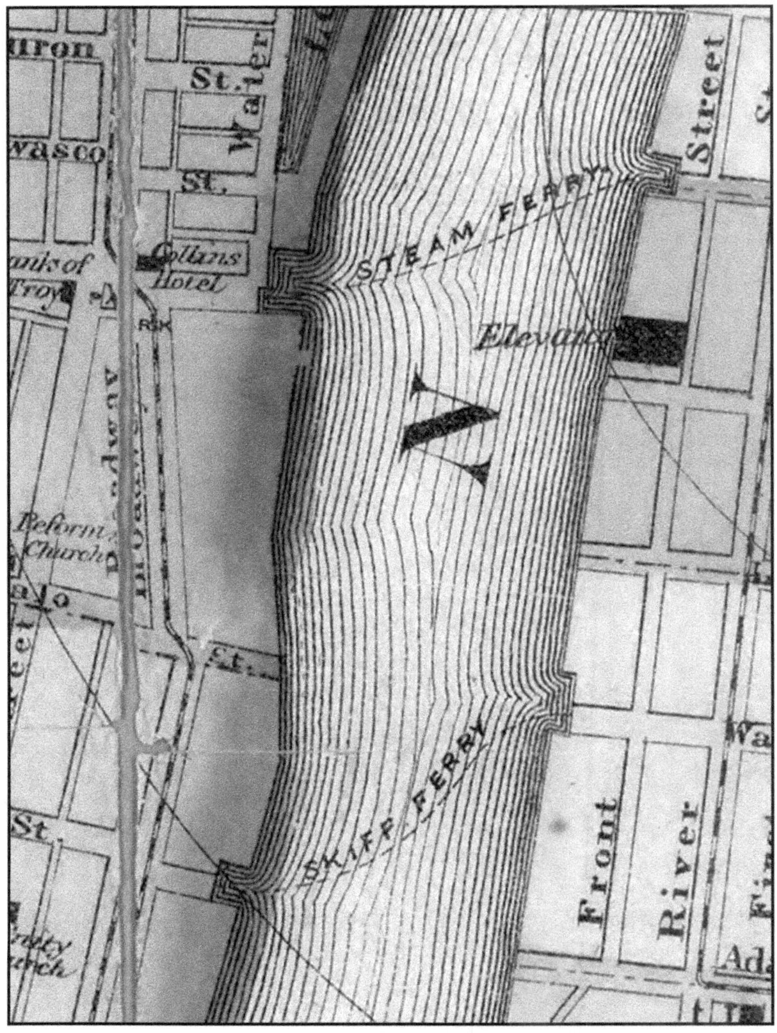

There were two ferries that went between Troy and West Troy in the 19th century. A skiff ferry went from Washington Street in Troy to Ferry Street (now 14th St.) in West Troy and a steam ferry from Ferry Street in Troy to Collins Hotel on Broadway. On May 11, 1907 the Frank W. Roosa Ferry operated by the West Troy Ferry Company broke its rudder and suspended trips. The Thomas Rath Ferry owned by the same company was being repaired in Roundout.

This is the steam ferry from Ferry Street in Troy to Collins Hotel on Broadway. Congress Street Bridge is behind and Ferry Street in Troy is to the right of the bridge. In June, 1915, the ferry service between Ferry Street in Troy and 16th Street in Watervliet, in operation for more than 70 years ended. Moved to the foot of Broadway.

Appears that the people are waiting for the Ferry boat that can be seen on the top right.

19th street and 12th ave looking east. Circa early 1900s. Notice the trolley coming up 19th. Tracks went south on 12th St past the high school and reconnected with Route 2 by St. Patricks cemetery due to the steep grade at 19th St.

Watervliet High graduates of 1938. 1245 Hillside Dr.

Original Watervliet High School.

Watervliet High School Library. Sylvia Inglee, Carol Rochford, Giselle Kuryatnik, Susan Wrzochalski, Paula Tybush, Elaine Goetz, Donna Shaughnessy and Gail Valentine. Part of the class of 1961.

School 1 around 1900.

School 3 in 1934. M. N. Mooney, Elizabeth L. Buckley, Elizabeth M. Grogan, Ada B Heenan, Leah M. Dorgan, Mary E. Farrell, Winifred A. Nolan, Mary I. Molony, Lena C. Wald, Irene M. Smith, Teresa Hillis, Helen Walsh, Marguerite L. Ryan, Margaret E. Lettis, Alice T. James, Mary Blaney, Thos. J. Costello, Mary T. O'Brien, Willard A. Hull, William Richmond, Irene Banski, Mary Putuluychck, Helen Stanchuk, Clara A. Jackson, Charlotte A. Byrnes, Ruth Hislop, Naomi Hunter, Lillian Perry, Mary Shumansky, Theresa Chuhta, Ruth Eckardt, Mary Kowalchick, Miriam Horton, Laura I. Veina, Collins Perry, Nicholas Fedonishinko, Arthur Van Antwerp, Frank Peters, Felix Prokrym, Edgar E. Alsey, Anvin Dellehunt, John Dugay, William Topkins, Robert Griffing, Stephen Antoniak, Earl Lester, Charles Rickenecker.

WHS Gym bag.

Our Lady of Mt. Carmel class of 1958.

Our Lady of Mt. Carmel K-2 class of 1948.

Sacred Heart of Mary 8th Grade in 1935.

St Patrick's class of 1944.

St Patrick's Garnet Athletic Club 1938 Softball Champions.

1st Ave & 14th Street United Methodist to the right. School 5 to the left. Bridge is gone today as well as the canal.

August 27, 1942, street scene in front of a neighborhood grocer.

September 13, 1942, street scene.

Frank DiNuzzo. 215 23rd St. DiNuzzo landed in New York City May 15, 1906, and resided in Stowe, PA., before coming to Watervliet in February, 1909, where he became employed by the West Side Structural Steel Co. He married in 1911 to the former Vincensa Razano. He later became building inspector for the City of Watervliet from Jan. 1, 1950 to Feb. 28, 1961. During his term as building inspector, Mr. DiNuzzo instituted a new and up-to-date filing system for recording the activities of his office. Mr. DiNuzzo served as a Democratic committeeman in the Third Ward, Second District. He also served as president of the Italo-Balbo Club. He died in 1970, age 80.

Frank Di Nuzzo. 215 23rd St. Notice the old style gas pumps and oil tanks. The Erie Canal ran in front of his shop. SOCONY was the merget of Vacuum Oil Company and Standard Oil Company of New York, commonly called Socony Oil to form the Socony-Vacuum Oil Company in 1931 and later would change the name to Mobil. Mobil in term merged with Standard Oil Company of New Jersey to form ExxonMobil in 1999. The original Vacuum Oil was founded in 1866 by Hiram Bond Everest and Matthew Ewing of Rochester.

Patrick Clement Simmons [birth name: Simoni] was a right handed relief pitcher. Played briefly for the Boston Red Sox during the 1928-1929 seasons. ERA was 3.67. Win loss record was 0-2. 18 strikeouts. He appeared in 33 games. Debuted with the Boston Red Sox on Oct. 6, 1929. His last year in ball was 1933, in four games for the Albany Senators. He was born in Watervliet on Nov. 29, 1908. Attended PS No. 7 but left after 8th grade. He enjoyed art and had his own sign shop at age 15. After baseball, he was a commercial artist and owned Simmons Signs and Simmons Store Fixtures and Neon, Inc. He died on August 3, 1968.

Two views of 2nd Ave. Switcmans Tavern is on the right in top photo. It was also known as the Silver Moon Bar.

Cartwrights. Between 23rd and 24th Streets. Franchised Ford dealers. 1940s-60s. Tag line: “Where Buying is Saving.”

Looking west from the East side of the Congress Street Bridge.

Unknown interior.

School #7. 6th Ave and 16th St.

St. Bridgets Fife & Drum. c. 1919. St. In 1923, the spelling of the name of the church was changed from St. Bridget to St. Brigid, apparently because it was believed to be the correct spelling of the Irish Saint to whom the parish was dedicated. After 161 years of service to the community, St. Brigid's Church was permanently closed in June 25, 2011. In March 2012 the church and school became the home of Wicked Smart, is a local, full service provider of apparel which includes screen printing, embroidery, custom T-shirts and has been in business since 2003.

One of Meneely's largest cast bells, all 7,000 pounds of it, made for St Patrick's Church. The bell was rescued when Price Chopper destroyed the church for one of their new grocery stores. It had been ringing in the church since 1890. It now is in the possession of the Watervliet Historical Society.

State Bank of Albany on the Southwest corner of 19th St. and Broadway. 1950s. Demolished. State Bank was founded in 1803. Became Norstar but Norstar was gone by 1987.

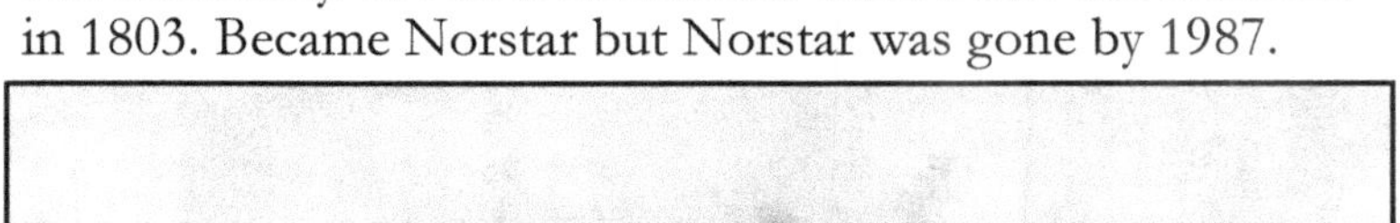

View of West Troy in 1848 from Mt Ida, Troy.

Watervliet Branch of the State Bank of Albany
Broadway & 19th St.

The bank was a landmark seen coming over the Congress Street Bridge from Troy for many years. Nothing to see now after the new Congress Street Bridge demolished it all.

Demolition of the bank on Broadway and 19th St. Taken from the Congress Street Bridge.

Thomas Joseph Donovan (January 1, 1873 – March 25, 1933). Major League Baseball outfielder who played for one season for the Cleveland Blues (18 games) from Sept 10 to Sept 28, 1901. Right handed outfielder. Batting average .254. 5 RBI's. His brother, catcher Jerry Donovan, also played in the majors with Philadelphia Phillies in 1906. Had .100 BA, RBI 15.

Jack O'Brien was an outfield and third baseman born in Watervliet on Feb 5, 1873. He played for three years in National and American League: 1899 and 1901 for the Washington Senators (NL & AL) and Cleveland Blues, and 1903 for the Boston Americans which finished first in the American League with a 91-47 season, and won the World Series 5-3 over the Pittsburgh Pirates. He ranked 9 out of the top 12 players. Had a .210 batting average. Cy Young pitched in that series. It was only the third season for the new franchise which later became the Boston Red Sox. The manager was Jimmy Collins and its home games were at Huntingon Avenue Grounds. O'Brien died June 10, 1933, at age 60 in Watervliet. His overall career batting average was .259 with 9 home runs. In 1899 he ranked 10th in homeruns with 6 in the National League and in 1903 ranked 16th with 3 homeruns in the American League. His RBI total was 133. His most productive season came in 1899 as a rookie debuting on April 14, 1899, for the Washington Senators, when he hit .282 and reached career-highs in home runs (6), RBI (51), runs (68), stolen bases (17) and games played (127). But he is best remembered as the first player to pinch-hit in a World Series game. He struck out for Boston catcher Lou Criger in the 9th inning of Game One of the 1903 series against Pittsburgh.

The Watervliet Colonial Club at 1582 Broadway. See next page for history.

Colonial Club. 1582 Broadway. Originally built as the YMCA by the Troy YMCA in 1892 then in 1898 the building was taken over by The Watervliet Club made up of merchants and businessmen of the city and used it as a social club. A few years later when the Watervliet Club dissolved it was taken over by the Colonial Club, made up of the wealthier residents of the city, and the members were known as the "Social 400." In 1910 the Masonic Temple Association bought the building, which had been next door on the second floor at 1592-94 Broadway. The Colonial Club had bowling tournaments and dancing. The April 20, 1911, Troy Times reported: *"The Fate of the Club. Whether the Colonial Club, for years prominent in the social life of Watervliet, will continue for another year, or go out of existence is one of the questions to be decided at the annual meeting of the club Monday night. One ticket only has been posted for the election of officers, and so greatly has the interest in the club died out among the members that its future is very uncertain. In case the Colonial Club disbands the Indications are that the Masons will take the rooms for social purposes."* The next day: *"Social Club to Continue. The Colonial Club last night decided to continue, and received assurances of a large number of new members. The Ghost Club, nearly thirty strong, desired to join the Colonial Club—not as an organization, but as individual members. As the Colonial Club has been considerably depleted during the last year by deaths and resignations, the new members will be a most welcome addition to its strength. A committee was appointed to confer with the Ghost Club before taking any further action. The annual reports received showed that the club was not in debt. These officers were elected: President. Benjamin W. Knower; Vice President, Charles F. Folk: Treasurer, John L. Haswell; Secretary. Leyt S. Bibbins; Board of Governors, Frederick W. Carl and Harry M. Hulsapple."*

The Ghost Club, composed of a coterie of young men of the city, whose professional abilities as actors and vocalists are recognized by the community, their entertainments being of a high order. President, Geo. F. Jamison; treasurer, Edward B. Shires; secretary, Alonzo Roush; tenor, Edwin H. Billings.

From *History of the City of Watervliet, N.Y.* 1910.

Behr Manning Plant. Sold to Norton Co. in 1931.

MANNING, John Alexander, industrialist, was born in Troy, N.Y., June 29, 1869, son of John Alexander and Mary Bowers (Warren) Manning, grandson of William Henry and Susan Perrine (Morrison) Manning, and great-grandson of Henry and Betsy Manning, who came to this country from England. John A. Manning was educated at the Troy Academy and was a student at Williams College for a year (1887). Upon leaving college he went into the family business which had been founded by his grandfather in Troy, N.Y., in 1846, for the manufacture of rope manila paper in a building which later became part of the Mount Ida Mill. His grandfather died in 1855 and was succeeded by the subject's father (q.v.) who effected a change in the partnership in 1857, its title becoming Manning & Peckham. In 1866 the Olympus Paper Mill was started in Troy with E. Warren Paine, and in 1883 the Crystal Palace Mill, which was operated alone under the elder Manning. The subject be-came president of the company at the death of his father in 1900 and the John A. Manning Paper Co. was organized to centralize the management and operation of the three properties. He re-maimed as president until the close of his life. In 1915 it was necessary to build a new mill to replace the Olympus and Crystal Palace mills due to the loss of water rights to the federal govern meat. The Green Island Mills Corp. was formed and a mill built on Green Island. In 1923 it was merged with the John A. Manning Paper Co. Inc., and continued under the latter name. In 1928 the Manning & Peckham Co., comprising the Mount Ida Mill, was merged with the paper company. The company's growth and increased standard of quality made it a leading source of supply in this country and in many foreign countries. In the course of time the company manufactured paper to be used as backing of sandpaper or coated abrasives. With Lewis S. Greenhead, Manning acquired land and machinery and built a plant in Waterville, N.Y. In 1912 the plant was finished and became the Manning Sandpaper Co. Six years later the name was changed to the Manning Abrasive Co., Inc. In 1928 it was merged with Herman Behr & Co., of Brooklyn. N.Y., becoming the Behr-Manning Corp., with factory and offices in Watervliet, and in 1931 it became a subsidiary of the Norton Co., Worcester, Mass. Manning was president of the Manning Abrasive Co., Inc., and later of the Behr-Manning Corp., and a director of the Norton Co. until his Death. In addition to his interest in the paper industry, Manning was active as a member of the board of directors of the New York Telephone Co., The International Purchasing Co., and the United National Bank (later the National City Bank) of Troy. He was a director of Trinity Institution Inc., Albany, N.Y., a welfare organization, and of Albany Medical College, and was a trustee and member of the finance committee of the Troy YMCA. He was especially interested in the Albany Hospital and served as its president from 1932 to 1937 and as a member of its board of governors from 1937 until his death. He was a member of Kappa Alpha and belonged to the Schuyler Meadow Country Club, the Old Chatham Hunt Club, the Troy (N.Y.) Country and Troy clubs, the Fort Orange Club of Albany, the Clove Valley Rod & Gun Club, near Poughkeepsie, N.Y., and the Oakland (SC) Club. Politically he was an independent Republican. His chief recreations were golf, fishing, fox hunting, shooting, and polo. He was married in Ballston Spa, N.Y., Oct. 11, 1900, to Edith Helen, daughter of Benjamin Franklin Baker of that place, who had extensive lumber interests in Canada, and had two daughters: Edith Baker, who married Lewis Stone Greenleaf, Jr., and Shirley Bowers, who married Serge Putative. His death occurred in Loudonville, N.Y., Mar. 15, 1938.

THE NATIONAL CYCLOPEDIA OF AMERICAN BIOGRAPHY

John A Manning

Advertisement and catalog entries for Berh-Manning abrasives. They made sandpapers, garnet cloth, and other abrasives. H. Behr & Co made sandpaper in Brooklyn in 1883 before merging with Manning Abrasive Co in Troy in 1928. See article on Behr here: https://www.waltergrutchfield.net/behr.htm

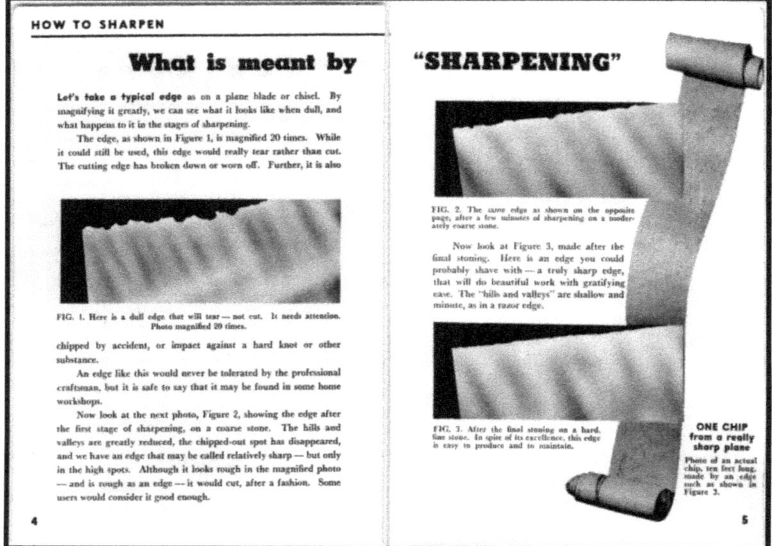

HOW TO SHARPEN

What is meant by "SHARPENING"

Let's take a typical edge as on a plane blade or chisel. By magnifying it greatly, we can see what it looks like when dull, and what happens to it in the stages of sharpening.

The edge, as shown in Figure 1, is magnified 20 times. While it could still be used, this edge would really tear rather than cut. The cutting edge has broken down or worn off. Further, it is also chipped by accident, or impact against a hard knot or other substance.

FIG. 1. Here is a dull edge that will tear — not cut. It needs attention. Photo magnified 20 times.

An edge like this would never be tolerated by the professional craftsman, but it is safe to say that it may be found in some home workshops.

Now look at the next photo, Figure 2, showing the edge after the first stage of sharpening, on a coarse stone. The hills and valleys are greatly reduced, the chipped-out spot has disappeared, and we have an edge that may be called relatively sharp — but only in the high spots. Although it looks rough in the magnified photo — and is rough as an edge — it would cut, after a fashion. Some users would consider it good enough.

4

FIG. 2. The same edge as shown on the opposite page, after a few minutes of sharpening on a moderately coarse stone.

Now look at Figure 3, made after the final stoning. Here is an edge you could probably shave with — a truly sharp edge, that will do beautiful work with gratifying ease. The "hills and valleys" are shallow and minute, as in a razor edge.

FIG. 3. After the final stoning on a hard, fine stone. In spite of its excellence, this edge is easy to produce and to maintain.

ONE CHIP from a really sharp plane

Photo of an actual chip, ten feet long, made by an edge such as shown in Figure 3.

5

Brownies Motorcycles and Sherlock's Grill at Broadway and 16th Street. Sherlock's founded by Bob Sherlock as one of the first sports bars. Pat Riley and Bob Lanier and other basketball locals went there. Said to have had the best Ham Sandwich.

Brownies and Sherlocks, 16th and Broadway.

White Eagle Bakery. 2428 4th Ave. 1950s. Founded in 1927 by John Bania at 2438 4th Ave. It was a small baking room with a brick oven and small retail shop. A horse and buggy made deliveries. A fire destroyed the place and he moved to 2428 4th Ave. For years he made house to house deliveries. In 1949 Ted Bania, his son, took over and by 1962 he employed 120 people in 12 retail stores around the Capital District.

Ohio Street Methodist Church. 3rd Ave and 21st St. Now St Annes, circa 1880s. The towers were added in the 1890s. This church was organized in the spring of 1849 by Alexander S. Lobdell, Ashael Potter, Edward Mallory, R. E. Gorton and Otis Wood. On June 5, 1849, the trustees of this church purchased the church property located on the Southwest corner of Ohio and Ontario streets in this village, known as the First Presbyterian or Congregational Church, and commonly called the "Bethel Church." This church edifice was a small wooden structure and on Nov 19, 1849 was totally destroyed by fire. The first preacher assigned to this congregation was the Reverend I. F. Yates. Immediately after the destruction of the "Bethel," this congregation took action to rebuild the church, and in the following spring (1850) the corner-stone of the present church edifice was laid, and the building was completed soon after, which is a two-story brick structure, the auditorium being on the second floor and the Sunday school and class rooms on the first floor. For about thirty years this church was the only Protestant church in the northern part of this village. In 1881 the brick parsonage, which adjoins this church on the South, was erected.

D&H with replica Stourbridge Lion Steam Engine. Last time this replica was fired up was in the 1930s. The famous Lion, the first locomotive to operate for commercial purposes in North America, made its historic ride in Honesdale, Pennsylvania on August 8, 1829.

According to Peter Becker, *"The locomotive was built for the Century of Progress Exposition in Chicago in 1933 from original blueprints, by the Delaware & Hudson (D&H) Railroad Company. In 1941, the replica was acquired on permanent loan by the Wayne County Historical Society and housed in a structure on Park Street. Operated at that time for the exposition, the replica also was exhibited at the 1939-40 World's Fair in New York City. The locomotive made to order in the late 1820's in Stourbridge, England, for purchase by the D&H Canal Company. The D&H created the town of Honesdale as the head of its 108 mile canal, designed to ship anthracite coal to market. That experiment failed, in that the hemlock rails were deemed inadequate for the 14,000 pound engine (and hauling a 5,800 pound tender). It nevertheless was later recognized as the first commercial use of a steam engine on a rail on this continent, hailing the birth of a new age of transportation and industry. Eventually disassembled, surviving pieces were donated to the Smithsonian Institution in Washington, D.C."*

Gallaghers Fish Fry, circa 1940, on Broadway looking east. George A. Gallagher was a former professional baseball player. He gave up this building and built an A-frame next to the Arsenal on Third Ave in 1970. Father and son ran it until the creation of I-787 next to it which hurt the business and it was sold in the late 1990s. George died in 2003. The building is now used by a different venture. Best fish fry!

C. B. Harris Auto Shop.

Broadway looking south one block south of Congress St.

William P. Carr was a Nash Car Dealer. The Nash 400 was a series of six-cylinder cars from the Nash Motors Company in Kenosha, Wisconsin. It was only manufactured in the 1936 model year and was sold in the line up between the smaller LaFayette and the larger Ambassador. The 400 DeLuxe *Model 3640A* was introduced on 15 October 1935. Technically, it was similar to the 400 but had a grille with chromed vertical bars and a split hood, as well as better equipment. In 1937, both models were replaced by the Nash LaFayette.

THEODORE ROOSEVELT.

Copyrighted, 1906, by D. WATSON, Watervliet. N. Y.
Tune—Hail to the Chief.

Flash went the tidings, o'er land and o'er ocean,
When Peace did triumph, and war had an end.
Thanks to our Chieftain, who 'mid the commotion,
Stepp'd in the breach as counsellor and friend.
His was a noble part,
Showing a manly heart,
Bravely he did his best peace to restore.
Then shout with best intent,
God bless our President.
Theodore Roosevelt, thee we adore.
Theodore Roosevelt, thee we adore.

When brave McKinley, cut off 'mid his glory,
No longer could steer the good Ship of State,
Then found we one who's now famous in story
Holding her steady, nor yielding to fate.
Thus did our noble Chief
Come to our great relief.
Showing a courage that calm did restore.
Steering through Panama,
Respecting God and Law.
Theodore Roosevelt, thee we adore.
Theodore Roosevelt, thee we adore.

We're glad the nations are singing thy praises,
Earth is delighted to honor thy name;
Your's is a stren'ous life that ever raises
One that doth right to the Temple of Fame.
We do thy name revere,
And would it loudly cheer
'Till spheres far away re-echoes it o'er
With gifts so full and free.
Yes, we are proud of thee.
Theodore Roosevelt, thee we adore.
Theodore Roosevelt, thee we adore.

No. 8.

Theodore Roosevelt, by D. Watson. Watervliet, N. Y. 1906.

First Baptist Church, 16th and 3rd Ave.

Looking north on Broadway from north end of Arsenal, 1950s.

Watervliet Baseball team. Some made it to the big leagues.

Patrick Henry "Paddy" Ryan (1851–1900) was a saloonkeeper and bare knuckle American boxer from Troy who won the worlds heavyweight-boxing championship from Joe Goss in 1880. He owned a saloon in the famous Watervliet "Sidecut." He was elected into the Boxing Hall of Fame in 1973.

www.ingramcontent.com/pod-product-compliance
Lightning Source LLC
LaVergne TN
LVHW052346100826
845147LV00012B/765

* 9 7 8 0 9 3 7 6 6 6 6 4 7 *